MADE WITH EDAM
DUTCH EDAM – REDDY FOR ANYTHING

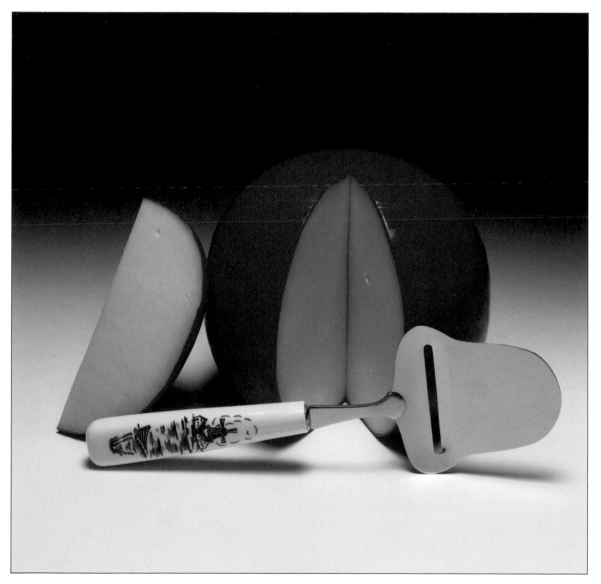

Colour Library Books

INTRODUCTION

Cheese is one of the most natural and convenient foods available. It can be eaten just as it is, or used as an ingredient in a whole manner of different dishes. Cheese also provides many of the nutrients, such as protein, fat, vitamins and minerals, which are essential to keep the body functioning efficiently.

The Dutch have been producing and exporting cheese for centuries and Edam actually takes its name from the town where it was first produced around 700 years ago. At one time all Dutch cheese was made on farms in the lush pasturelands of North and South Holland and Friesland, but industrialisation means that today, cheese is made in computerised creameries all over The Netherlands. The Dutch take the quality of their cheese very seriously. A government control stamp placed on every cheese ensures it is easy to trace when and by whom any single cheese was made, thus guaranteeing that whichever part of country the cheese originates from, the flavour and texture are always of a consistently good quality.

It is not surprising to discover then that Edam has long been Britain's favourite foreign cheese. As well as being of a consistently high standard, it contains only 90 calories per ounce, and as it is made from skimmed milk, it is low in fat. Edam is also extremely versatile – it slices, grates and cubes perfectly, it does not crumble like most other popular hard cheeses and its mild flavour enhances, rather than obscures, the delicate tastes of contemporary favourites such as fish, fruit and vegetables.

This exciting collection of recipes from The Dutch Dairy Bureau provides a wealth of ideas on how to liven up your mealtimes by combining Edam with other delicious and wholesome ingredients. Most of the recipes also include Dutch unsalted butter, as, contrary to popular belief, butter contains no more calories than margarine, and, of course, it tastes so much better.

Each recipe has been calorie counted so that you can make the appropriate choice for your own, and your family's eating plan. All the dishes are healthy, yet satisfying enough to disguise the fact that you may be watching your family's weight as well as your own. A number of the recipes are without meat or fish and so can also be enjoyed by vegetarians.

Edam is now available nationwide in handy wedges, and pre-packed slices are also becoming more readily obtainable. So go ahead and try these imaginative recipes and you will soon discover why Dutch Edam is the tastiest, most versatile cheese you can buy.

CLB 2687
© 1991 Colour Library Books Ltd., Godalming, Surrey.
Printed in Singapore.
All rights reserved.
ISBN 0 86283 867 3

The cheese girl symbol is the internationally registered
trademark of the Dutch Dairy Bureau.

PARSLEYED EDAM TERRINES

Serves 4 at 290 Kcals per serving

This light, low-calorie terrine is a great favourite and will especially appeal to weight watchers.

2 eggs (size 2 or 3), lightly beaten
2 tbsps Greek cow's yogurt
25g/1oz parsley, finely chopped
Black pepper
4 tbsps fresh breadcrumbs
300g/10oz Edam, grated
½ small carrot, peeled
French flat leaf parsley to garnish

Sauce
6 tbsps water
3 tbsps natural yogurt
1 tbsp tomato purée
¼ tsp ground cumin

1. Combine eggs, yogurt, parsley, pepper, breadcrumbs and Edam together and stir well.

STEP 1

2. Cut the carrot into thin rings, arranging 3-4 overlapping in the bottom of 4 lightly oiled 150ml/¼-pint ramekins.

STEP 2

3. Divide the mixture between the ramekins and place in a pan of hot water to come no more than halfway up the side of the dishes.

STEP 3

4. Cover the pan with foil and a lid, reduce the heat and simmer for 8 minutes, or until set.

5. Prepare the sauce by bringing the 6 tbsps water to the boil, remove from heat and add the yogurt, purée and cumin. Set aside.

6. When the terrines are cooked, pour off any excess liquid and run a sharp knife round the edges of the terrines. Leave to stand for 1 minute then unmould onto hot serving plates and pour sauce around the terrine. Garnish with the parsley before serving.

Cook's Notes

TIME: Preparation takes about 15 minutes and cooking takes 8 minutes.

COOK'S TIP: If ramekin dishes are unavailable, try cooking the mixture in an egg poacher. Breadcrumbs are easily made in the food processor, and any surplus can be frozen in plastic bags and used straight from the freezer.

HAM AND EDAM SPIRALS

Serves 4 at 225 Kcals per serving

An indulgent starter which can be made well in advance of that special occasion.

200g/7oz Edam, coarsely grated
200g/7oz carton plain quark (skimmed milk soft cheese)
1 tbsp finely chopped spring onion
Cayenne pepper
6 slices lean ham
Sprigs of chervil for garnish

1. Mix the Edam and quark together in a food processor or blender to form a paste.

STEP 1

2. Add the spring onion and a couple of pinches of cayenne pepper to taste, and allow processor to run briefly.

3. Lay the slices of ham on a board and spread generously with the Edam mixture.

4. Roll the ham slices lengthways into thick rolls.

STEP 4

5. Wrap the rolls in foil and chill in the refrigerator for 2 hours, or until filling is firm.

6. Just before serving, carefully slice the rolls and arrange on 4 small plates. Serve immediately, garnished with sprigs of chervil

STEP 6

Cook's Notes

⏱ TIME: Preparation takes 15 minutes and chilling takes 2 hours.

🍴 COOK'S TIP: The rolls will keep well in the refrigerator so can be prepared the day before they are required.

◯ SERVING IDEA: Ideal served as canapes with drinks. The filling could also be used as a topping on toast.

❓ VARIATION: The quark could be replaced with curd cheese, although this will increase the calories.

SMOKED HADDOCK AND EDAM GRATIN

Serves 4 at 506 Kcals per serving

A classic appetizer which also makes a hearty family meal when prepared in a large dish.

25g/1oz Dutch unsalted butter
25g/1oz plain flour
300ml/½ pint milk
1 tsp mustard powder
1 tsp lemon juice
175g/6oz Edam, grated
Freshly ground black pepper
225g/8oz smoked haddock, cooked, boned and
　flaked
200g/7oz can sweetcorn, drained
450g/1lb cooked, mashed potato

Garnish
Lemon slices
Sprigs of dill

1. Make sauce by placing the butter, flour and milk into a saucepan and whisking over a gentle heat until thick and smooth. Continue cooking for 2 minutes.

STEP 1

2. Add mustard powder and lemon juice, and gradually stir in the Edam. Season to taste.

3. Add smoked haddock and sweetcorn to the sauce.

STEP 3

4. Divide the mixture between 4 scallop shells or heatproof dishes. Pipe a border of potato around the edge of the scallop shell.

STEP 4

5. Place under a low grill for 10 minutes until the top is golden brown.

6. Garnish with lemon slices and sprigs of dill.

Cook's Notes

⏱ TIME: Preparation takes about 30 minutes and cooking takes 10 minutes.

❓ VARIATION: For a change substitute 175g/6oz cod and either 50g/2oz prawns or mussels for the haddock, or a mixture of your choice. For a supper or lunch dish pour the fish sauce into one large buttered ovenproof dish. Instead of covering with mashed potato, use crushed potato crisps.

Bake in a moderate oven for 10-15 minutes to heat through.

🍳 COOK'S TIP: The smoked haddock could be cooked in the milk to be used for the sauce, either in a saucepan or in the microwave.

✳ FREEZING: Open freeze then wrap. Defrost 4-5 hours in refrigerator and heat through in the oven.

MINTED EDAM SOUP

Serves 4 at 217 Kcals per serving

A fresh, light summer soup – ideal for outdoor entertaining.

25g/1oz fresh mint, chopped
25g/1oz fresh parsley, chopped
2 cloves garlic, crushed
150ml/¼ pint thick, Greek yogurt
1 tbsp lime or lemon juice
150ml/¼ pint iced water
Salt and black pepper
150g/5oz cucumber, diced
175g/6oz Edam, diced

Garnish
4 sprigs fresh mint

1. Place the first five ingredients in a blender or food processor and blend to a smooth purée. If a processor is not available, whisk until evenly blended. Add iced water and blend again. Season to taste.

STEP 1

2. Mix together the cucumber and Edam and pile some into the centre of each soup dish.

STEP 2

3. Carefully pour the soup around the cucumber and Edam and garnish with mint.

STEP 3

Cook's Notes

⏱ TIME: Preparation takes about 15 minutes.

◣ PREPARATION: If you do not have a garlic press, slice the garlic thinly, sprinkle some salt over and leave for a few minutes. It should then crush easily.

❓ VARIATION: Alternatives to mint or parsley – spring onion or chives and dill. The Greek yogurt can be replaced by natural set yogurt if preferred, or natural fromage frais.

PASTEL PATÉ EDAM

Serves 4 at 272 Kcals per portion

Made in minutes, this easy-to-prepare pâté also makes a tasty sandwich filling.

300g/10oz kipper fillets, cooked, skinned and
 flaked
225g/8oz Edam, grated
2 tsps finely grated lemon rind
4 tbsps lemon juice
2 tbsps boiling water
Freshly ground black pepper

Garnish
Curly endive or cos lettuce
French flat leaf parsley sprigs

STEP 1

Flaking the fish

1. Place all the pâté ingredients in a food processor or blender and mix to a paste. Chill for 15-20 minutes.

2. Using an ice cream scoop dipped in hot water and dried, form the pâté into ball shapes. Garnish the pâté with sprigs of parsley and serve on a bed of lettuce, accompanied by Melba toast.

STEP 2

Cook's Notes

⌊ TIME: Preparation takes 15 minutes.

❓ VARIATION: Use smoked mackerel instead of kipper fillets.

◯ SERVING IDEA: Instead of using a scoop, the pâté could be piped in a large

rosette on each dish. Use a large bag and a star nozzle.

✱ TO FREEZE: Pack into a rigid container, freeze for 1 month. Thaw in container for 6-8 hours or overnight.

EDAM SALAD FEUILLETTES

Serves 4 at 395 Kcals per serving

An unusual, crisp starter or tempting snack which will win you many compliments.

225g/½lb puff pastry
A little beaten egg or milk for brushing
40g/1½oz lambs lettuce, washed and trimmed
8 cherry tomatoes, cut into quarters
75g/3oz Edam, cut into batons
50g/2oz alfalfa sprouts (optional)
1 avocado
Few drops lemon juice

Dressing
3 tbsps natural fromage frais
1 tbsp white wine vinegar
2 tbsps white grape juice
3 tbsps chopped chives
Celery salt and pepper to taste

1. Roll out the pastry into a rectangle 11x26cm/4¼x10¼ inches. Trim off the edges and cut into 4 pieces each 10x6cm/4x2½ inches. Mark a rectangle ½cm/¼ inch in from the edge of each, cutting through the pastry only the slightest

STEP 1

fraction. Brush the top of each feuillette with beaten egg or milk. Chill for 10 minutes.

2. Preheat the oven to 220°C/425°F/Gas Mark 7.

3. Bake the feuillettes on a lightly moistened baking tray for about 15 minutes or until well risen and golden brown.

4. Remove the centre of each feuillette and carefully scoop out and discard any soft pastry from the inside. Set the lids to one side, return the bases to the oven for a few minutes more to dry out. Cool on a wire rack.

STEP 4

5. Mix together the lambs lettuce, tomatoes, Edam batons and alfalfa sprouts. Divide between the feuillettes.

6. Halve, stone and peel the avocado and cut into thin slices lengthways. Sprinkle lemon juice over to prevent discolouration.

7. Mix together the dressing ingredients until well blended. Spoon some over the filling in each feuillette and arrange the avocado slices across the top. Place the pastry lids on top.

Cook's Notes

⏱ TIME: Preparation takes 25 minutes, cooking takes 15-20 minutes.

❓ VARIATION: Lambs lettuce is also sometimes called Corn Salad. If unavailable it can be replaced by watercress.

❗ WATCHPOINT: Do not put the filling into the pastry until just before serving, so that the pastry remains crisp.

👨‍🍳 COOK'S TIP: The pastry cases can be made beforehand and stored in an airtight container or wrapped in foil and frozen, then crisped up quickly in a hot oven when needed.

SAVOURY CROISSANTS

Serves 4 at 238 Kcals per serving

Want a quick, easy, yet delicious snack - try these unusual, filled croissants.

4 croissants
15g/½oz Dutch unsalted butter
2 sticks celery, coarsely chopped
75g/3oz button mushrooms, sliced
½ small green pepper, diced
50g/2oz Edam, grated
Watercress to garnish

STEP 2

1. Preheat oven to 150°C/300°F/Gas Mark 2 and heat the croissants through.

2. Melt the butter in a heavy-based pan over moderate heat. Stir in the celery, mushrooms and green pepper, cover and cook gently for 5 minutes until just tender. Remove from heat and stir in the grated Edam.

3. Split the croissants open lengthways, then sandwich together with the savoury filling. Return to the oven for 5 minutes, then serve garnished with watercress.

STEP 2

STEP 3

Cook's Notes

TIME: Preparation takes 15 minutes, plus 5 minutes cooking.

VARIATION: Grated Edam combined with chopped onion, flaked, poached haddock and a little Greek yogurt is a delicious alternative filling. For a really speedy snack, split the croissant, fill with a generous slice of Edam, and bake until cheese begins to melt.
Croissants could be substituted with small pitta breads.

TO MICROWAVE: Place celery, mushrooms and pepper in a basin and flake on the butter. Microwave on HIGH for 1½ minutes, stir in the grated Edam and cook on HIGH for 30 seconds more. Split open and fill the croissants. Place on a microwave-proof plate and cook on HIGH for 1 minute. Stand 1-2 minutes before serving.

EDAM PIZZA SNACKS

Makes 12 slices at 72 Kcals each

A tasty snack – delicious as a cocktail nibble or for a more substantial lunchtime snack, use slices of wholemeal bread.

---

1 baton or ½ French stick, about 25cm/10-inches long
1 large clove garlic (optional)
2 tbsps tomato purée
100g/4oz Edam, cut into triangles
50g/1¾oz can anchovy fillets, drained
6 black olives, halved
Oregano or basil

---

1. Cut the bread into 12 thin slices. Peel the garlic clove, and rub over the top of each slice if desired.

STEP 2

3. Halve the anchovy fillets and arrange in a criss-cross pattern on top of each. Garnish with halved olives and a sprinkling of herbs.

STEP 1

2. Spread each slice of bread with a thin layer of tomato purée and top with a triangle of Edam.

STEP 3

4. Put under a medium grill until cheese begins to melt. Serve immediately, garnished with extra herb sprigs.

Cook's Notes

L TIME: Preparation takes 15 minutes, plus 5 minutes cooking time.

◣ PREPARATION: For a less salty flavour, soak the anchovy fillets in milk for 5 minutes before using.

? VARIATION: For a children's alternative, use tomato ketchup instead of purée, and replace anchovy and olives with strips of ham or bacon and small slices of tomato. For a more substantial snack either of these toppings could be used on slices of wholemeal bread.

EDAM FILO PURSES

Serves 4 at 290 Kcals per serving

These filo purses are easy to prepare and make a perfect start to any meal, or a tasty snack.

100g/4oz small leeks, sliced into rings
225g/8oz Edam, cut into 1cm/½-inch cubes
4 tbsps mango chutney
4 sheets filo pastry (defrosted if frozen)
25g/1oz Dutch unsalted butter, melted

Garnish
Lollo Rosso lettuce leaves and tomato

STEP 4

1. Preheat oven to 200°C/400°F/Gas Mark 6.

2. Blanch leeks in boiling water for 1 minute and drain.

3. Mix Edam, leeks and chutney together in a bowl.

5. Divide mixture evenly between each cross and place in the centre. Gather up pastry ends over filling, secure with string and frill out pastry.

STEP 3

4. Cut each sheet of filo pastry into quarters to give 16 rectangles. Brush half of these with melted butter and place other half on top. Then lay one double over another to make a cross. Repeat four times.

STEP 5

6. Place on baking sheet and bake for 15-20 minutes until golden brown. When cooked, remove string and serve garnished with lettuce and tomato.

Cook's Notes

⌛ TIME: Preparation takes about 30 minutes and cooking takes 15-20 minutes.

◯ SERVING IDEAS: A delicious starter, light summer lunch or part of a buffet meal.

SPRING VEGETABLES WITH EDAM AND NUT DIP SAUCE

Vegetables serve 4-6 persons at 464-310 Kcals per serving
Dip serves 8-10 persons at 232-185 Kcals per serving

This attractive presentation of fresh spring vegetables makes a most sophisticated appetizer for 4 persons. Alternatively it looks and tastes great with cocktails.

100g/4oz baby sweetcorn, washed
100g/4oz mange tout, trimmed
225g/½lb young carrots
4 spring onions

Dip
2 slices bread, crusts removed
75g/3oz Edam, grated
50g/2oz flaked almonds, roasted
50g/2oz salted cashew nuts
1 small carton natural low fat yogurt
1 tbsp walnut or hazelnut oil
5 tbsps corn or sunflower oil
Juice of ½ lemon
Salt and cayenne pepper to taste

1. Boil the baby sweetcorn and mange tout in lightly salted water for 3-4 minutes. Drain and refresh under cold running water. Drain well. Scrub the carrots and cut into fingers if too large.

STEP 2

2. Cut the green stalks of the spring onions in fine rings (save the white bulbs of the onions for another dish).

3. Lay the bread in a bowl and soak in 2 glasses of water.

STEP 3

4. Put the Edam, almonds and cashews into a food processor and mince fincly. Squeeze the water from the bread and add to the mixture with the yogurt, two oils and lemon juice, and blend to a thick sauce. Add salt and cayenne pepper to taste. Chill for half an hour.

5. To serve as a starter, arrange the vegetables in a colourful ring around individual plates, then spoon some of the dip into the centre. Sprinkle the onion rings over. Serve the remaining dip in a separate bowl. To serve as a party dip, place the dip in a bowl with the vegetables arranged on a large plate around the bowl. Sprinkle the onions over the dip and then sprinkle with cayenne pepper.

Cook's Notes

TIME: Preparation takes 20 minutes, chilling takes 30 minutes.

PREPARATION: To roast almonds, place in heat-proof dish or tin and bake in a moderate oven until golden brown – about 15 minutes.

VARIATION: The vegetables can be replaced by strips of green or red pepper, celery or savoury biscuits.

WATCHPOINT: Although the vegetables can be prepared in advance, the dip should be served almost immediately after chilling.

VEGETABLE MEDLEY

Serves 4 at 510 Kcals per serving

Simple ingredients are used to greatest effect in this easy-to-prepare dish.

50g/2oz Dutch unsalted butter
1kg/2lbs potatoes, peeled
225g/8oz onions, skinned
275g/10oz Edam, coarsely grated
1 green pepper, seeded and chopped
1 red pepper, seeded and chopped
Black pepper
15ml/1 tbsp chopped parsley to garnish

1. Melt the butter in a large, heavy-based frying pan.

2. Slice the potatoes and onions very thinly.

3. Place the potatoes, onions, Edam and peppers in alternate layers in the pan, seasoning well between each layer and finishing with a layer of Edam.

STEP 3

4. Cover with a piece of foil, and cook over a gentle heat for 35-40 minutes, until cooked. Serve sprinkled with chopped parsley.

STEP 2

STEP 4

Cook's Notes

TIME: Preparation takes about 20 minutes and cooking 35-40 minutes.

COOK'S TIP: New potatoes with the skin left on add extra flavour. Can be made in a shallow, greased ovenproof dish – fry potatoes and onions in butter, then layer up in dish with cheese and pepper. Cover with foil, bake at 200°C/400°F/Gas Mark 6 for 40-50 minutes.

ITALIAN VEGETABLE SALAD WITH EDAM

Serves 4 at 270 Kcals per serving

This unusual salad can be served as a starter at a dinner party or as a delicious lunchtime dish.

1 stick celery, cut into 1cm/½-inch slices
¼ fennel, cubed
50g/2oz mange tout, cut into 1cm/½-inch pieces
8-12 broccoli florets
¼ cucumber
4 cooked artichoke hearts, thinly sliced (optional)
2 tbsps pine kernels
175g/6oz Edam, cut into matchsticks
8-12 black olives
1 tbsp chopped chives

Dressing

2 tbsps extra virgin olive oil
Few drops lemon juice
1 small clove garlic, crushed
1 tbsp pesto (basil sauce)
Salt, pepper, sugar to taste

STEP 2

1. Blanch the celery, fennel, mange tout and broccoli. Drain and immediately refresh under cold running water and allow to drain well.

2. Cut the cucumber in half lengthways, remove the pips with a teaspoon, and then slice.

3. Place all the vegetables in a bowl, reserving the olives and chives.

4. Mix the olive oil with a few drops of lemon juice, the crushed garlic and pesto. Season to taste.

5. Spoon the dressing over the vegetables and mix carefully and well. Allow the salad to stand for about 20 minutes in a cool place (but not in the refrigerator) so that the vegetables can absorb the dressing.

6. Brown the pine kernels in a frying pan on a medium heat, shaking and turning them continuously.

7. Mix the Edam matchsticks carefully through the vegetable salad and divide between 4 plates.

8. Garnish with the olives, browned pine kernels and chopped chives. Do not allow to stand too long before serving.

Cook's Notes

TIME: Preparation time 30 minutes, standing time 20 minutes.

VARIATION: Alternative to pine kernels: flaked almonds or sunflower seeds. These could also be browned in a moderate oven.

WATCHPOINT: Add vegetables to already boiling water and do not allow

them to boil for more than 4-5 minutes or they will lose their crispness.

BUYING GUIDE: Pesto sauce is available in small jars in most large supermarkets.

ECONOMY: A small can of artichoke hearts can be substituted for the fresh artichokes.

EDAM GRATIN

Serves 4 at 366 Kcals per portion

Low in calories, yet nutritious, Edam Gratin makes a wonderful lunch or supper dish.

225g/8oz broccoli florets
225g/8oz French beans, sliced
450g/1lb spinach, roughly torn
15g/½oz Dutch unsalted butter
1 large ripe avocado, skinned and cubed
Salt and pepper
175g/6oz Edam, grated
75g/3oz bran biscuits, crushed
1 tsp sesame seeds

1. Blanch the first three vegetables in boiling salted water until just tender. Drain and pile into a hot buttered gratin dish. Add avocado and toss together. Season to taste.

2. Mix the Edam, biscuit crumbs and sesame seeds together and sprinkle over the vegetables.

STEP 2

3. Place the dish under a hot grill until the cheese bubbles.

STEP 1

STEP 3

Cook's Notes

[icon] TIME: Preparation takes about 15 minutes plus 5 minutes grilling.

[icon] MICROWAVE: The vegetables could be blanched in the microwave for about 4 minutes if desired.

[icon] SERVING IDEA: Perfect as an accompaniment to fish or egg dishes, or as a main course with crisp French bread or rolls.

EDAM AND PASTA SALAD

Serves 4 at 205 Kcals per serving (without dressing)

An easy-to-prepare pasta salad which is ready in minutes.

100g/4oz pasta twists, cooked and cooled
100g/4oz Edam, cut into 1cm/½-inch cubes
1 small green pepper, cored, seeded and sliced
1 small red pepper, cored, seeded and sliced

Dressings
Equal quantities of vinaigrette dressing and
   natural fromage frais with added curry
   powder to taste.

or

2 tbsps extra virgin olive oil
Few drops lemon juice
1 small clove garlic, crushed
1 tbsp pesto
Salt, pepper and sugar to taste

Cut the Edam into cubes.

1. Combine the first four ingredients in a bowl, and dressing, if used, tossing lightly to mix well.

STEP 1

2. Place in a serving dish. Chill and serve.

Mix the pasta to prevent it sticking together.

Cook's Notes

⏱ TIME: Preparation takes about 15 minutes.

❓ VARIATION: A good salad for using up leftover vegetables, fruit, meat or fish, i.e. broccoli, mange tout, orange, melon balls, tuna, prawns, ham, salami.

EDAM HEALTH SALAD

Serves 4 at 228 Kcals per serving

A simple yet nutritious salad, delicious as a main meal especially when watching the calories.

1 medium red onion, skinned and sliced into rings
1 Spanish onion, skinned and sliced into rings
2 oranges
225g/8oz Edam, cut into 1cm/½-inch cubes

Dressing
4 tbsps orange juice
2 tsps olive oil
Black pepper
12 black olives
Sprigs of fresh mint

1. Place onion rings in large bowl and blanch for 1-2 minutes in boiling water. Drain, refresh in iced water, and drain again.

STEP 1

2. Remove the zest from the oranges, slice finely and reserve. Slice away and discard the pith and slice the oranges into rings.

STEP 2

3. Arrange a border of onion rings on a large serving plate, and inside this a circle of orange slices.

STEP 3

4. Mix the Edam with the dressing ingredients and orange zest and pile into the centre of the oranges. Garnish with olives and mint sprigs.

Cook's Notes

TIME: Preparation takes about 25 minutes.

VARIATION: If you cannot obtain red onions use sliced tomatoes instead.

COOK'S TIP: Use a vegetable peeler to remove the zest thinly.

COURGETTE AND EDAM AU GRATIN

Serves 4 at 327 kcals per serving

Served on its own or as an accompaniment to meat or fish, this dish is a winner for anyone who is watching the calories.

50g/2oz Dutch unsalted butter
1 large onion, sliced into rings
1kg/2lbs courgettes, sliced into 1cm/½-inch
    pieces
Salt and black pepper
1 tsp oregano
225g/8oz Edam, grated
Chopped parsley for garnish

1. Preheat oven to 190°C/375°F/Gas Mark 5.

2. Melt the butter in a large frying pan and gently cook the onion until softened and transparent.

STEP 3

4. Season with salt, freshly ground black pepper and the oregano. Stir thoroughly.

5. Place the vegetables in a shallow ovenproof dish and sprinkle with the Edam cheese.

STEP 2

3. Add the courgettes and continue cooking for 10 minutes, turning the vegetables over occasionally.

STEP 5

6. Cover with foil and bake in the preheated oven for 20 minutes. Remove the foil and cook for a further 10 minutes. Serve sprinkled with chopped parsley.

Cook's Notes

⤺ TIME: Preparation takes 20 minutes and cooking takes 30 minutes.

◯ SERVING IDEAS: Serve with meat or fish, or on its own as a light lunch or supper dish.

EDAM AND VEGETABLE STIR-FRY

Serves 4 at 183 Kcals per serving

Edam cheese gives extra body to this Chinese-style dish with a good blend of colours, flavours and textures.

450g/1lb mixed crisp vegetables (choose from
  sliced leeks, courgettes, sweet peppers, green
  beans, florets of cauliflower or broccoli,
  julienne of carrots or parsnips)
15g/½oz Dutch unsalted butter
1 tbsp sesame or sunflower oil
½ tsp cumin seeds (or ground cumin)
½ tsp ground coriander
½ tsp garam masala
Finely grated zest and juice of 1 large orange
100g/4oz Edam, cubed
4 spring onion curls for garnish

1. Prepare, wash and dry the vegetables.

STEP 1

2. Heat the butter with the oil in a large wok or frying pan over a medium heat. Add the vegetables and spices and stir-fry for 2 minutes.

STEP 2

3. Add the orange zest and juice to the pan and bring to the boil. Reduce heat to low and simmer 3-4 minutes until the vegetables are barely tender. Add the Edam and stir-cook for 30-40 seconds until heated through and beginning to melt. Serve immediately, garnished with spring onion curls.

STEP 3

Cook's Notes

⏱ TIME: Preparation takes 15 minutes and cooking takes 8-10 minutes.

❓ VARIATION: Give this stir-fry a stronger Chinese flavour by substituting finely grated root ginger for the spices and adding a dash of soy sauce with the orange juice.

❗ WATCHPOINT: Do not allow to stand after adding Edam.

EDAM AND TROUT CEVICHE

Serves 4 at 270 Kcals per serving

Definitely a must for low calorie dining. This unusual combination of ingredients not only looks good but tastes wonderful.

175g/6oz fresh rainbow trout fillets, cut into
    small strips
4 tbsps lemon or lime juice
225g/8oz Edam, cubed
25g/1oz fresh coriander roughly torn
1 x 100g/4oz mango, skinned and cubed
Sea salt and freshly ground green peppercorns
2 large heads of chicory

1. Place the fish and lime or lemon juice in a non-metallic bowl. Leave to stand for 2-3 hours in a refrigerator or until fish has turned pale.

STEP 1

2. Add Edam, coriander leaves and mango and season to taste.

STEP 2

3. Arrange chicory leaves, radiating outwards around the edge of the serving dish. Pile the fish and Edam mixture into the centre and pour juice over the top.

STEP 3

Cook's Notes

🕐 TIME: Preparation takes about 20 minutes, standing time is 2-3 hours.

❗ WATCHPOINT: Refrigerate if not serving immediately and serve within one hour.

◯ SERVING IDEA: Serve with crisp, brown bread rolls.

DUTCH AUBERGINE BAKE

Serves 4 at 350 Kcals per serving

The unusual combination of vegetables and Edam cheese produces a light and delicious main meal.

450g/1lb aubergines
15g/½oz unsalted Dutch butter, melted
450g/1lb leeks, thinly sliced
225g/8oz Edam
1 small carton natural, low-fat yogurt
Salt and freshly ground black pepper
100g/4oz lean bacon, lightly grilled and cut into
    thin strips
1 tsp oregano

1. Preheat oven to 220°C/425°F/Gas Mark 7.

2. Cut aubergines into 1cm/½-inch thick slices and place on a lightly buttered baking sheet. Brush the slices with the melted butter and bake for 15 minutes.

STEP 2

3. Blanch the leek slices in boiling salted water for 1 minute, then drain.

4. Arrange half the aubergine slices in a shallow ovenproof dish and cover with half the leeks. Grate half of the Edam and sprinkle over.

STEP 4

5. Pour over the yogurt, sprinkle on seasoning to taste and repeat the layers of vegetables.

6. Put a ring of bacon in the centre. Cut the remaining Edam into triangles and arrange around the bacon. Sprinkle the oregano over, and return to the oven for 20 minutes until the Edam has melted.

STEP 6

Cook's Notes

⏱ TIME: Preparation 20 minutes and cooking 20 minutes.

🍳 TIP: This dish can be prepared in advance, kept refrigerated and then baked when required.

◯ SERVING IDEA: Serve with baked jacket potatoes. For a vegetarian dish just omit the bacon.

CAULIFLOWER CHEESE DUTCH STYLE

Serves 4 at 335 Kcals per serving

A popular family favourite – quick to make as well as nourishing.

1 large cauliflower
25g/1oz unsalted Dutch butter
25g/1oz plain flour
280ml/½ pint skimmed milk
175g/6oz Edam, grated
1 small onion, skinned and cut into rings
175g/6oz back bacon, grilled, then cut into strips
Salt and pepper

Garnish
Chives
Paprika

1. Trim cauliflower and break into florets. Wash and cook in boiling water for about 15 minutes.

STEP 1

2. Make a sauce by placing butter, flour and milk into a saucepan and whisking continuously over a gentle heat until thick and smooth. Add the grated Edam, onion rings, and seasoning to taste.

STEP 2

STEP 2

3. Place cauliflower and bacon in a serving dish. Pour the cheese sauce over. Garnish with chives and paprika before serving.

Cook's Notes

⌙ TIME: Preparation takes about 20 minutes.

🍳 COOK'S TIP: Stir the sauce carefully once the onion rings have been added to ensure that they retain their shape.

? VARIATION: The bacon can be replaced with sliced Dutch smoked sausage or ham.

CHICKEN IN CIDER

Serves 4 at 515 Kcals per serving

This is an economical main course which the whole family will enjoy.

50g/2oz streaky bacon, cut into strips
1 medium onion, diced
100g/4oz button mushrooms, quartered
350g/12oz ripe tomatoes, skinned and chopped
1 clove garlic, crushed
20g/¾oz Dutch unsalted butter
20g/¾oz flour
280ml/½ pint cider
1 small green pepper, deseeded and sliced
1 small red pepper, deseeded and sliced
450g/1lb cooked chicken, cubed
½ tsp dried or 1 tsp fresh chopped thyme
Salt and pepper

Topping

450g/1lb mashed potatoes
50g/2oz Edam cheese, finely grated
Sprigs of thyme to garnish

1. Lightly fry the bacon, then add the onion and mushrooms and fry until brown. Drain on absorbent paper.

STEP 1

2. Cook the tomatoes and crushed garlic to a rich pulp.

3. Meanwhile, put the butter, flour and cider into a saucepan, heat gently, stirring or whisking continuously until the mixture boils and thickens.

4. Blanch the pepper and add to the tomato pulp and continue cooking for 3-5 minutes.

5. Preheat the oven to 190°C/375°F/Gas Mark 5.

6. Stir the chicken, bacon, onion and mushrooms into the tomato mixture with the thyme and seasoning to taste. Place in a large ovenproof dish. Season the cider sauce and pour over the chicken.

7. Season the mashed potato and add the finely grated Edam. Place in a large piping bag with a large star nozzle. Pipe a border of potato over the chicken.

STEP 7

8. Bake in preheated oven for 30-40 minutes. Serve immediately garnished with thyme sprigs.

Cook's Notes

⏱ TIME: Preparation takes about 35-40 minutes and cooking takes 30-40 minutes.

❗ WATCHPOINT: Do make sure the Edam is finely grated or it will block up the nozzle and make piping difficult.

✳ FREEZING: Open freeze to avoid squashing potato rosettes. Wrap well. Freeze 2 months. Best frozen before baking.

❓ ECONOMY: The fresh tomatoes could be replaced by a well drained 400g/14oz can of tomatoes.

EDAM BALLETJES

Serves 4 at 480 Kcals per serving

This dish originates from Holland, and is best served with vegetables or salad to make a hearty family meal.

40g/1½oz fresh breadcrumbs
3 tbsps water
450g/1lb lean pork, minced
1 tbsp made mustard
2 tbsps fresh parsley, finely chopped
175g/6oz Edam, grated
1 dessertspoon fresh, mixed herbs
1 egg (size 3 or 4), beaten
Salt and black pepper
5g/¼oz unsalted Dutch butter
150ml/¼ pint dry red wine
450g/1lb leeks, diagonally sliced
4 carrots, diagonally sliced
Parsley sprigs for garnish

STEP 3

STEP 6

1. Soak the breadcrumbs in the water for 5 minutes. Mix with the minced pork in a large mixing bowl.

2. Add the mustard, parsley, Edam, herbs, egg and seasoning. Mix together thoroughly.

3. Form the mixture into 20-25 small balls and refrigerate for 30 minutes.

4. Preheat the oven to 180°C/350°F/Gas Mark 4.

5. Grease a large ovenproof dish with the butter, put the balls in a single layer and bake in preheated oven for 15 minutes.

6. Pour the wine over and continue baking for a further 30 minutes.

7. Meanwhile, cook the leeks and carrots together in boiling salted water until just tender, then drain and keep warm.

8. Arrange the vegetables around the edge of a large serving dish, and pile the balletjes and sauce into the centre. Serve immediately, garnished with parsley.

Cook's Notes

TIME: Preparation takes 30 minutes, chilling 30 minutes and cooking 45 minutes.

VARIATION: The minced pork can be replaced with minced chicken or beef.

COOK'S TIP: The balletjes will reheat well in the oven if covered, but check they are reheated thoroughly before serving.

FREEZING: Open freeze the balletjes before the cooking stage, and pack into containers or freezer bags when solid. Freeze for no more than 1 month.

ITALIAN FISH BAKE

Serves 4 at 195 Kcals per serving

Try this recipe for white fish – livened up with Edam, fennel, tomatoes and anchovies, it is sure to be a success with all the family.

450g/1lb white fish fillets, skinned
15g/½oz Dutch unsalted butter
1 tbsp lemon juice
Salt and pepper
1 tbsp fresh fennel, chopped
75g/3oz Edam, thickly sliced
2 tomatoes, sliced
8 anchovy fillets
2-3 black olives, halved and pitted
Fresh dill sprigs for garnish

---

1. Preheat the oven to 200°C/400°F/Gas Mark 6. Trim the fish into serving portions.

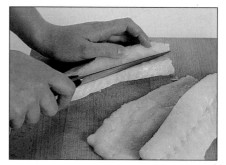

STEP 1

2. Use half the butter to grease a shallow ovenproof dish and arrange the fish in a single layer. Sprinkle with lemon juice, seasoning and fennel. Cover loosely with buttered foil and bake for 15 minutes.

STEP 2

3. Arrange the cheese over the fish and top with tomato slices, anchovy fillets and halved olives. Re-cover and bake for 10 minutes more. Serve garnished with dill.

STEP 3

Cook's Notes

⏱ TIME: Preparation takes 10 minutes, cooking takes 25 minutes.

❓ VARIATIONS: If preferred, the anchovy fillets can be replaced by strips of green pepper. To give the dish a French flavour use a little basil and ratatouille spooned over the fish, top with the cheese slices.

◎ SERVING IDEA: Serve with a green salad, tossed in a good French dressing.

📟 TO MICROWAVE: Cover dish loosely with greaseproof paper and cook on HIGH for 3 minutes. Add the topping and cook, uncovered for 2 minutes more.

DUTCH CHICKEN SLICE
Serves 6 at 270 Kcals per serving

If you don't know what to do with left-over chicken try this Dutch slice. It's delicious either hot or cold.

350g/12oz cooked chicken, minced
100g/4oz fresh white breadcrumbs
½ level tsp mustard powder
1 large onion, finely chopped
50g/2oz mushrooms, finely chopped
175g/6oz Edam, finely grated
½ level tsp celery salt
1 level tsp finely grated lemon rind
2 level tbsps fresh parsley, chopped
2 eggs (size 2 or 3), beaten
100ml/4 fl oz milk
1 tsp Worcestershire sauce
Salt and freshly ground black pepper

Garnish
Cucumber twists
Slices of radish
Lollo Rosso lettuce leaves
Parsley sprigs

1. Preheat the oven to 180°C/350°F/Gas Mark 4.

2. Mix together the chicken, breadcrumbs, mustard, onion, mushrooms, Edam, celery salt, lemon rind and parsley. Stir in eggs, milk and Worcestershire sauce, and season to taste.

3. Spoon the mixture into a greased 1kg/2lb loaf tin, and smooth top with a round-bladed knife.

STEP 3

4. Bake in the centre of pre-heated oven for 1 hour, until firm.

5. Leave to cool for 5 minutes before turning out.

STEP 2

STEP 5

Cook's Notes

TIME: Preparation time is about 25 minutes, cooking takes 1 hour.

SERVING IDEAS: Delicious as part of a packed lunch or picnic. Serve hot with a piquant sauce and crunchy green vegetables or cold with your favourite salad.

FREEZING: Wrap well in polythene and freeze for up to 1 month. Thaw in wrapping for 6-8 hours or overnight in refrigerator.

TEXEL PLAICE

Serves 4 at 334 Kcals per serving

Dispensing with the usual cheese sauce makes this substantial fish dish very calorie kind.

450g/1lb fresh spinach or 1 x 225g/8oz packet
    frozen, whole leaf spinach
20g/¾oz Dutch unsalted butter
Salt and freshly ground black pepper
4 x 225g/8oz plaice fillets, skinned
100g/4oz Edam, cut into 8 thin slices
175g/6oz button mushrooms, finely sliced
65ml/2½ fl oz dry cider

Topping
2 tbsps fresh breadcrumbs
½ tsp paprika
Parsley sprigs to garnish

---

1. Wash and trim the fresh spinach, cook in a saucepan awithout extra liquid for approximately 5 minutes. Drain well. Alternatively, cook frozen spinach following the directions on the packet. Stir the butter into spinach and season.

STEP 1

2. Preheat the oven to 190°C/375°F/Gas Mark 5.

3. Cut each plaice fillet in half lengthwise, and season. With skinned side uppermost, cover each piece of fillet with a slice of cheese, mushrooms and the spinach.

STEP 3

4. Fold each end to the centre and place in an ovenproof dish with the joins underneath. Pour over the cider and then sprinkle over the breadcrumbs and paprika.

STEP 4

5. Bake in preheated oven for 20 minutes. Garnish with parsley before serving.

Cook's Notes

🕐 TIME: Preparation takes 25 minutes, cooking takes 20 minutes.

❓ VARIATION: Use apple juice or white wine instead of cider. Can be prepared in advance, without the topping, covered and refrigerated, then completed and cooked when required.

◎ SERVING IDEAS: Serve with small new potatoes or a crisp green salad.

CHICKEN MARSALA

Serves 4 at 425 Kcals per serving

A special dish that looks as though it should be complicated but is, in fact, surprisingly simple to prepare.

4 chicken breasts
Seasoned flour
50g/2oz Dutch unsalted butter
100g/4oz button mushrooms, sliced
2 tsps flour
100ml/4 fl oz dry white wine
3 tbsps Marsala wine
100ml/4 fl oz natural fromage frais (8% fat),
Salt and pepper
75g/3oz Edam cheese, cut into 4 slices

Garnish

25g/1oz flaked almonds, toasted
Chopped fresh parsley

1. Remove skin and bones from chicken breasts, and coat in seasoned flour.

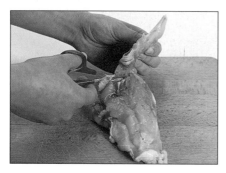

STEP 1

2. Melt the butter in a large frying pan, fry the chicken breasts gently for about 15-20 minutes, turning occasionally, until golden brown and cooked through. Remove from the pan, place on a flame-proof serving dish and keep warm.

STEP 2

3. Sauté the mushrooms in the remaining butter in the pan and add to the chicken.

4. Sprinkle in the flour, cook for one minute, and gradually add the white wine and Marsala. Bring to the boil, stirring constantly. Add the fromage frais and reheat. Add seasoning to taste.

STEP 4

5. Pour sauce over the chicken, place slices of Edam on top of the chicken. Brown under a hot grill. Sprinkle with toasted almonds and parsley to garnish.

Cook's Notes

⏱ TIME: Preparation takes approximately 20 minutes and cooking takes 15-20 minutes.

❗ WATCHPOINT: To avoid curdling, do not allow the sauce to boil after adding the fromage frais.

⭕ SERVING IDEA: Serve with boiled rice and a crisp green vegetable such as French beans.

◆ BUYING GUIDE: Look out for pre-skinned and boned chicken breasts in the supermarket.

APPLES FILLED WITH NUTS AND RAISINS

Serves 4 at 180 Kcals per serving without sauce
210 Kcals per serving with sauce

The ingredients may be simple, but the finished dish makes an elegant conclusion to a family meal or dinner party.

2 cooking apples
1 egg, size 4 or 5, beaten
75ml/3fl oz natural low fat yogurt
15g/½oz caster sugar
Juice of ½ lemon
50g/2oz Edam, finely grated
1 tbsp coarsely chopped walnuts
2 tbsps raisins
Pinch of cinnamon
Sprigs of mint for decoration

Sauce (optional)
1 mango or 225g/½lb fresh apricots
½ tsp lemon juice
5g/1 heaped tsp caster sugar

1. Cut the apples in half and carefully remove the core. With a pointed spoon, carefully hollow out about half of the apple. Cut the apple removed from the hollowed out halves into small pieces.

STEP 1

2. Preheat oven to 150°C/300°F/Gas Mark 2.

3. Mix beaten egg in a bowl with the small pieces of apple and all the other main ingredients.

4. Fill the hollowed-out apples with this mixture.

STEP 4

5. Place in an oven-proof dish and cook in the preheated oven for 30 minutes, until the filling is firm.

6. Allow to cool and serve decorated with sprigs of mint and with, or without, the sauce.

7. To prepare the sauce, cut the peeled mango or apricots down the centre and remove stones. Cut the fruit into pieces and purée to a smooth paste.

8. Press the paste through a fine sieve and flavour with lemon juice and sugar to taste.

9. Spoon the sauce onto 4 dessert plates and place the filled apples in the centre. Serve immediately.

Cook's Notes

TIME: Preparation takes 20 minutes, cooking takes 30 minutes with 10 minutes for the sauce.

VARIATION: The raisins and walnuts could be replaced by 3 tbsps of mincemeat.

ECONOMY: The fresh apricots could be replaced by canned, drained apricots, but omit the sugar.

TIP: Try to pick cooking apples with a rosy tinge to add colour.

LEMON EDAM DIP WITH FRUIT CRUDITÉS

Serves 4 at 200 Kcals per serving

An easy, light dessert to make, which is also easy on the waistline.

Dip
100g/4oz Edam, finely grated
3 tbsps boiling water
175g/6oz natural fromage frais (8% fat)
2 tsps apricot jam
Grated rind of 1 lemon
1 tsp ground ginger

Fruit
Small amounts of at least four different fruits, e.g. grapes, strawberries, cherries and peaches
1 large green and 1 large red apple, cored and cut into 20 segments - dip in lemon juice to prevent browning.

1. Place the grated Edam in a bowl, add the boiling water, stir and add the fromage frais, apricot jam, lemon rind and ginger.

STEP 1

2. Spoon the dip into a glass dish and chill for 30 minutes.

STEP 2

STEP 1

3. Arrange decoratively on a serving plate with the fruit crudités as desired.

Cook's Notes

⏱ TIME: Preparation takes 25 minutes plus 30 minutes for chilling.

❓ VARIATION: Serve with crisp biscuits such as brandy snaps, instead of the fruit. Other suitable fruits include pears, melon, kiwi, pineapple, and mango.

ST CLEMENT'S CHEESECAKE

Serves 6-8 at 760 or 570 Kcals per serving

We all indulge in treats from time to time, but this sumptuous cake is not as naughty as it may appear.

Biscuit Base
100g/4oz Dutch unsalted butter
200g/8oz digestive biscuits, crushed
1 tsp mixed spice

Filling
1 packet lemon jelly
1 egg (size 3), separated
140ml/¼ pint skimmed milk
Rind and juice of 1 lemon
Rind and juice of 1 orange
225g/8oz Edam, finely grated
25g/1oz caster sugar
280ml/½ pint double cream

Decoration
Orange and lemon slices

1. Melt the butter in a saucepan, add the crushed biscuits and mixed spice, and mix well. Press the mixture into a 20cm/8-inch loose-based cake tin. Chill until ready for use.

STEP 1

2. Dissolve jelly with 2 tbsps hot water in a bowl over a saucepan of hot water. Beat together the egg yolk and milk and pour into jelly, stirring well. Heat for a few minutes without boiling. Remove from heat and add the lemon and orange rind, juice and Edam cheese, and liquidize or blend until thick and creamy. Cool just to setting point.

3. Beat egg white until stiff, add the caster sugar and whisk again.

4. Whisk half the cream until it holds its shape and gently fold the egg white and cream into the cheesecake mixture. Pour over the biscuit base and chill until firm and set. Can be frozen in the tin at this point (see Cook's Notes). When set, run a warmed knife around the edge of the cheesecake to remove from the tin.

STEP 4

5. Whip the remaining cream and pipe rosettes round the top of the cheesecake. Decorate with lemon and orange slices.

Cook's Notes

⏱ TIME: Preparation takes about 40 minutes.

🍲 COOK'S TIP: Use a potato masher to press biscuit base into cake tin for a smooth, even base.

❓ VARIATION: For a change use crushed ginger biscuits instead of digestive biscuits.

✳ FREEZING: Wrap well. Can remain frozen for up to 2 months. Take the cake out of the tin before defrosting.

VERSATILE EDAM

Dutch Edam is Britain's favourite foreign cheese – it's easy to slice, grate, cut into batons or cubes, and as Edam has a smooth, firm texture it does not crumble like most other popular hard cheeses.

Edam's mild flavour also means it combines well with both savoury and sweet ingredients. On this page we show a variety of fast and easy serving suggestions which don't need recipes, simply a list of the ingredients used, starting in the top right-hand corner:

1. Wholemeal brown bread cut into circles and topped with lettuce, Edam triangles and sliced tomatoes; red and green peppers with Edam triangles garnished with dill; rings of red onion interleaved with Edam triangles and topped with watercress.

2. Parma ham wrapped around Edam sticks.

3. Fruit salad of your choice with cubed Edam served with a dressing of 1 tbsp sunflower oil mixed with 1 tbsp raspberry vinegar or, if you prefer, just on its own.

4. Baked potatoes are extra delicious when served with grated Edam and then grilled for 30 seconds.

5. Asparagus or celery wrapped in thinly sliced Edam.

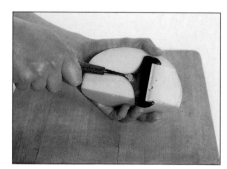

STEP 5

6. Small batons or sticks of Edam dipped in parsley and paprika.

STEP 6

7. Circles, cubes and triangles of Edam topped with tomatoes and olives, mushrooms and carrots, radish, green pepper and silver onions.

STEP 7

8. Soup, either home-made or from a tin, becomes extra nutritious and tasty with grated Edam sprinkled on top.

There are many more ways of serving Edam – by making sure you have a wedge always to hand in the fridge – Dutch Edam is reddy for anything.

Index

Photography by Peter Barry
Recipes Prepared and Styled by Helen Burdett
Designed by Judith Chant
Edited by Jillian Stewart